LIVE BOLDLY

WORKBOOK

EPISODES 16-30

BY: NICKI CORINNE WHITE

LIVE BOLDLY

LIVING INTENTIONALLY
IN TODAY'S WORLD
WORKBOOK
EPISODES 16-30

Published by Carpenter's Son Publishing, Franklin, TN
Scripture quotations are taken from
the New American Standard Bible,
Copyright © 1960, 1962, 1963, 1968,
1971, 1972, 1973, 1975, 1977, 1995
by The Lockman Foundation
Used by permission. (www.Lockman.org)
Front cover artwork by Nicki Corinne White
Interior design by Debbie Manning Sheppard
Printed in the United States of America

DEDICATION

Have you ever worked on projects that seem to go along fine, but then have some details that are tough for you to resolve? That is the way writing books is for me. I am an ideas person. I have literally dozens of ideas floating around in my head all the time. I know… it's not always a good thing. It is how I am wired, and how God made me. I am terrible at all the little details. And I am not a perfectionist. It is easy for me to miss something, or I basically just say it does not matter. I can shrug it off easily. But it can not be that way when writing a book. That is why people have editors. I have had an amazing editor for all my books: my friend, Tammy Kling, who is stellar at what she does, which is many things. You should google her. Too many things to count. For these three workbooks, we decided to have our edit team, from LIVE BOLDLY Ministries, work on them. They edit blogs, marketing material, canva posts, graphics, and websites. They did a fabulous job on the first workbook, and now on this workbook I am simply overwhelmed with gratitude. I have had so many irons in the fire, and they waited patiently while I finished up each chapter, and then worked on the many problems and holes which needed filling.

A special shout out to Maureen Loeffler, known to all of us as Re. She has worked for months on fine tuning, and even writing several of the questions. I cannot thank her enough. She goes over and over each chapter. This is NOT something I am gifted at. Her attention to detail is crazy amazing.

Another shout out to my daughter, Jessica Everett. She is my executive admin. We meet at least once a week and go over dozens of emails, create canva posts for social media, and talk about the upcoming schedule. She solves a lot of my tech issues too. Which are many.

My son, Nathan, also helps me. I call him when I am at my wit's end about a tech issue, and he patiently walks me through it.

And my wonderful husband, Craig. He has great ideas and implements them. There is nothing better than being in ministry with one's spouse to encourage them.

We have 15 other team members who add to our ministry at Live Boldly Ministries. They each have a role and pray for this ministry as it grows. I am so thankful to them. And to my publisher, layout person, publicist. It takes so many people to create something special.

I dedicate this book to all who encourage me and work hard to make something happen for the kingdom.

LIVE BOLDLY MINISTRIES TEAM

- CRAIG WHITE - husband, tech support, video editor, graphics
- JESSICA EVERETT - daughter, executive administrator, scheduling, emails, social media, marketing, basically everything
- NATHAN WHITE - son, tech support
- MAUREEN LOEFFLER - editor, tech support, advisor
- JAMIE HUDSON - photographer, editor
- RUTHANNE BEDDOE - editor, spiritual advisor
- TORI LOEFFLER - social media
- LISA SHUMAKER - sister, Col 3:12 Ministries team, marketing
- AMY CRIST - assistant administrator
- ASHLEY TAYLOR - Col 3:12 Ministries team
- KAREN LAW - Col 3:12 Ministries team, libraries
- LINDA SARACOFF - photographer, social media
- GABRIELLE BOLIOU - special projects, prayer team
- JEANETTE DICKEY - prayer team
- NANCY JINDRICH - prayer team
- COURTNEY JORDAN - prayer team
- CINDY SMITH - prayer team
- PRISCILLA ROBINSON - prayer team
- JONI SULLIVAN BAKER - Buoyancy PR, She has encouraged me, been patient with me as a new author and been easy to approach with my many questions.
- Also my editor TAMMY KLING who gave me the great idea to do a video series and these workbooks. She is a worldchanger!

TABLE OF CONTENTS

INTRODUCTION

INTRODUCTION

INTRODUCTION

After I finished my book, **BOLD - Living Intentionally In Today's World,** I began a video series on my YouTube channel. It is a 45 episode series in which I encourage people in their walk of faith. I hope they will be inspired to do all things to bring glory to God, and also be able to share the gospel with those around them. The videos are short and one could listen to 3-4 at one time. I felt there needed to be a next step. My editor encouraged me to do a workbook. Having taught Bible studies for years, I knew 45 chapters would be overkill. I decided to do three workbooks, each having fifteen chapters. This way someone could use them in a group Bible study.

I waited to see the response from the first workbook before putting out the next. I am thankful people have enjoyed it so much that I am able to now complete the other two.

This workbook begins with ways to share the gospel and then develops into the "why" of sharing. What God intends for us and how we need to prepare our heart and mind to be able to serve. Why we need to serve and how this grows us as a believer. This workbook will also share examples of godly people who will inspire us to live our life with purpose in every step we take.

I hope you enjoy working your way through this book. It is my prayer that each of you grow in your faith and spread God's Word to those around you.

Find all the videos for this workbook on
YouTube@nickicorinnewhite7299
(episodes 16-30)

EPISODE 16

SHARING YOUR FAITH

PART 1

The bottom line with sharing your faith - spending time and getting to know someone is key. It is true that you cannot always do that, but listening to someone share their heart and understanding what they know about God can be very helpful. I have found that one of the best ways to begin sharing is for me to share about my own walk and how God drew me to Himself.

There are many ways to share your testimony but we are going to focus on two. A longer version for family or friends you have known for awhile, and a short version for someone you may come across and need to quickly share.

I want you to know that I am not saying this is the only way to share the gospel but it may give you a starting point. Your story of how you came to believe in Jesus (that He died on the cross and rose again to pay for your sin so that you can have a relationship with God) is unique and special. No one has a better testimony than anyone else. God chose you and me before we were born and knew what our life would be like. You just need to share.

QUESTIONS

1. Write out your testimony of how you came to Christ (including Bible verses) that you would share with someone close to you. Maybe it would take you 2-5 minutes to share with them.

_____

_____

_____

_____

_____

_____

_____

2. Write out a short version for someone you may meet on a plane or in a store or park. Use key aspects like - sin, God's holiness, Jesus, a Bible verse, believing, acceptance, prayer. 30-45 seconds to share.

_____

_____

_____

_____

_____

_____

3. *Look up 8-10 Bible verses to memorize that you can share. I am sure you may have your favorites. A few of mine are: Romans 10:9, Romans 3:23, Romans 6:23, Acts 16:31, Ephesians 2:8-9, James 2:10. But you can memorize your favorites. Write them out and carry them with you until you have them memorized.*

_____

_____

_____

_____

_____

4. *Make a list of people in your life that you believe do not know Jesus. Put the list in your Bible to pray for them each day. Mine is on a post-it note inside the flap. God is faithful. He is sovereign. He is continually at work. Do not be discouraged.*

_____

_____

_____

_____

_____

5. *In your daily prayer time ask God to give you opportunities to share your faith. One thing that inspires me is to read about missionaries and other believers giving hours each day for Jesus. It helps me to keep my life in perspective.*

_____

_____

_____

_____

EPISODE 17

SHARING YOUR FAITH

PART 2

THE BARRIER

We need to remember: God is the one who draws people to Himself. We don't. Many people are broken and have struggles, fears, hardships. They may not see their need to have a Savior. Or maybe they see Jesus as a cure for their problems, BUT they NEED to see Jesus as a cure for their sin. If they do not understand that they sin then they will not fully understand grace.

> So this lesson will take us a step back and remind you of what the Bible says about our separation from God.

QUESTIONS

1. **Many people may say to you that they believe there is a God. Remember James 2:19**

   "You believe that God is one. You do well, the demons also believe, and shudder."

   We need to not only believe there is a God, but to know that He is holy and that sin separates us from Him. Find three verses that talk about our sin and how it creates a barrier between us and God.

   _____

   _____

   _____

2. **When talking to people about God, you can't assume people know things - be clear and explain things. Keep it simple. Tell them of God's love, sin and separation, and Christ's death and resurrection. Look up the following verses. What do they say?**

   Psalm 14:3_____

   _____

   _____

   _____

   Isaiah 53:6 _____

   _____

   _____

   _____

   _____

Ephesians 2:8-9 _____

_____

_____

_____

Romans 8:1 _____

_____

_____

_____

3. **God loved us so very much He provided a bridge (Jesus) to cross that barrier. God's son who became man on earth so we can have life with God in Eternity. The Bible tells us in**

   Romans 10:9-10:

   > _"That if you confess with your mouth Jesus as Lord, and believe in your heart that God raised Him from the dead, you will be saved; for with the heart a person believes, resulting in righteousness, and with the mouth he confesses, resulting in salvation."_

   They must take that step. Do you have someone in your life you have been sharing with that needs to take the next step? Pray for them now and for an opportunity to share these verses with them.

   _____

   _____

   _____

   _____

   _____

4. **So now we have covered three of the five main points to share: your testimony, the barrier of Sin, and Jesus as the bridge. Write out what you would say to someone to this point.**

    Romans 1:16

    > "For I am not ashamed of the gospel, for it is the power of God for salvation to everyone who believe, to the Jew first and also to the Greek."

    _____

    _____

    _____

    _____

    _____

    _____

    _____

    _____

    _____

    _____

    _____

    _____

    _____

    _____

EPISODE 18

SHARING YOUR FAITH

PART 3 -

CLOSURE

We have talked about God providing His only son to bridge the gap. He loves us so much. Jesus is the only payment for our sin. We must admit to God we are a sinner, believe in Jesus and confess your faith in Jesus as Saviour and Lord.

I find that sometimes it is easier to give these facts but tougher to actually ask the person if they are ready to believe and follow Jesus. So let us take a look at this aspect of sharing the gospel.

QUESTIONS

1. **Do you ever wonder why you are not there to "catch the fruit"? Maybe you have shared the gospel with someone for years and they move away, and when you visit them they tell you they accepted Christ. First of all, we will not always be there to see those we have been sharing with or praying for become believers. However, I know that I am shy about following through in this, asking them if they want a relationship with Christ or if they want to hear more. Maybe it is a fear of rejection. I am not sure but let us pray for boldness in this. Because it is not about "me", it is about someone's eternity. So pray as you share.**

   Ephesians 6:19 says,

   > *"And pray in my behalf, that speech may be given to me in the opening of my mouth, to make known with boldness the mystery of the gospel."*

   Pray right now for the boldness to ask someone if they are ready to believe in Christ.

   _____

   _____

   _____

2. **We need every bit of equipping from the Spirit of God to purposefully share the Gospel. Understanding God's power and goodness helps with this.**

   Isaiah 45:7

   > *"The One forming light and creating darkness, Causing well-being and creating disaster; I am the LORD who does all these things."*

Romans 2:4

"Or do you think lightly of the riches of His kindness and tolerance and patience, not knowing that the kindness of God leads you to repentance?"

In the midst of hard times, God's plans are good. Share a time when you may have questioned this. What made you realize God's goodness?

_____

_____

_____

Are any of these verses ones you can incorporate into your plan to share God's good news with others? Which ones will you use?

_____

_____

_____

3. **Look up the following verses:**

Romans 1:16_____

_____

_____

I Corinthians 15:3-4 _____

_____

_____

Romans 6:22-23 _____

_____

_____

Romans 8:38-39 _____

_____

_____

Romans 10:9 _____

_____

_____

Mark 16:15-16 _____

_____

_____

4. **Romans 1:16 says,**

    "For I am not ashamed of the Gospel, for it is the power of God for salvation to everyone who believes, to the Jew first and also to the Greek."

    I love this passage because God gives us power and we should never be hesitant to share the Gospel.
    Galatians 6:9 tells us,

    "Let us not lose heart in doing good, for in due time we will reap if we do not grow weary."

Take a step this week. Write down something you can do this week to reach out to someone. A coffee date, a note or a phone call - anything.

_____

_____

_____

_____

_____

_____

5. **Read Romans 10:13-14.**

> *"for 'WHOEVER WILL CALL ON THE NAME OF THE LORD WILL BE SAVED.' How then will they call on Him in whom they have not believed? How will they believe in Him whom they have not heard? And how will they hear without a preacher?"*

This passage encourages me to share far and wide. God is the one who draws but He uses His people. He uses all of us. Get together in person or on the phone with a friend who is a believer and encourage each other to reach out. Send an encouraging note to someone. Today.

_____

_____

_____

_____

_____

_____

EPISODE 19

SHARING YOUR FAITH

PART 4

BEING BORN AGAIN

What creates the passion in us? Why do we feel that sense of urgency to share the gospel? What does it mean to be born again?

We are going to take a look at Nicodemus. Here is someone who had moved up the ranks in the Sanhedrin, the ruling council of Jewish leaders. He was a teacher of teachers; he is thought to be one of the most well known teachers in Israel. And yet, he longed to meet with Jesus. He was hearing of miracles happening and was searching for answers that would make sense. The fact that he doesn't even really "get it" always surprises me. In spite of all his studies, he did not really grasp the concept that the Messiah was coming or know what signs in the Old Testament would point to it.

This brings us to today's lesson - know your person you are sharing with and understand how they perceive being saved. They can have a lot of head knowledge like Nicode-mus, but that does not mean they understand anything.

QUESTIONS

1. Read John 3. Nicodemas was a Pharisee. He wanted to learn from Jesus. John 3 is an important passage for all of us. Why? Because it shows how we are made new. It shows God's plan. Our sins are wiped clean and God transforms us - changes our lives. How would you explain to someone that being born again has nothing to do with working to get points or favor with God? Especially someone who has spent their entire life believing they can earn their salvation. Use Scripture.

   _____

   _____

   _____

   _____

   _____

   _____

2. Jesus clearly points out that one must be born again. There is no way around it. And it is true, we feel the wind, we know it is there but we don't see it. It's hard to understand things we can't see or feel. We feel like we have to be accomplishing things that are tangible, but we need to have Jesus work in us. We cannot do it on our own. God will transform us. In what way have you personally struggled with trying to do something on your own? What have you done to overcome this?

   _____

   _____

   _____

   _____

   _____

3. *Now turn to Numbers 21:6-9. What does the bronze serpent being lifted up by Moses represent? Why does Jesus use this example when talking to Nicodemus?*

_____

_____

_____

_____

4. *If you haven't done it already, take a post-it note and write down all the people you are praying for or need to be praying for that you believe are not believers. Or maybe you have thought of more people since you started your list. Put the post-it in your Bible. You may need more than one post-it.*

Pray for
Mom
Jacque
Philip
Maria
Kerry
Juan
JiChan . . .

_____

_____

_____

_____

_____

5. *As we wrap up this series on sharing our faith I hope that you can put all the pieces together. Go back and review the different steps. Write out a brief outline of the steps you can take. Add Scripture references.*

_____

_____

_____

_____

_____

_____

EPISODE 20

GOD WORKING IN US

God wants us to be holy, in-dwelled and serving. With the Holy Spirit living in us, we should have that desire to serve. It is true that we can push Him aside and ignore His prodding or we just get too overwhelmed by life. There are things we can do to help us to stay on track. This lesson will hopefully inspire you to be more faithful.

QUESTIONS

1. **Read Hebrews 13:20-21.**

   "Now the God of peace, who brought up from the dead the great Shepherd of the sheep through the blood of the eternal covenant, even Jesus our Lord, equip you in every good thing to do His will, working in us that which is pleasing in His sight, through Jesus Christ, to whom be the glory forever and ever. Amen."

   Jesus will equip you. What "tools" does He give you?

   _____

   _____

   _____

   _____

   _____

2. **2 Timothy 2:15 is a favorite Bible verse many learn at a young age. Why? Because it is VITAL that we don't misinterpret scripture when we share. So always read the context around the verse so you understand fully what is being said. And always ask questions. What is being said? Why is it being said? To whom? And sometimes knowing location and timeframe also can help. In verse 7 it says,**

   "Consider what I say, for the Lord will give you understanding in everything."

   Yay! That is so encouraging.

What do you do to stay in God's Word? What are ways you have learned to study God's Word? What other verses encourage you to study His Word?

_____

_____

_____

_____

_____

3. *There is a quote by Dwight Moody, "If Jesus bore the cross and died on it for me, ought I not be willing to take it up for Him?". I am a list maker. I have to be, or I would do all the things I love to do and maybe not finish what I "should" be doing. What are things you do to keep on track? I like to think of it as spokes on a bike. Fellowship, Bible, Pray, Church. If one thing is missing then your tire goes flat. Draw a diagram of what your tire would look like. What are your "spokes" on your wheel?*

4. **Redeeming our time. Ephesians 5:16:**

    "making the most of your time because the days are evil."

    Read all of Ephesians 6. Paul is telling us in this chapter about the armor of God. If we have our armor, then it will help us withstand when evil comes. We are then strengthened. We are to be careful how we live and manage our time well. Write out some things you can do this week...

    _____

    _____

    _____

    _____

5. **Think about the times you do speak to people. Did they learn something more about Jesus? Are they encouraged to live more like Jesus? Did you listen and try to meet a need through prayer? Make it a goal to do one of these three things as you interact with others.**

    _____

    _____

    _____

    _____

6. **Identify a person or persons who encourages you. Who is it that inspires you to live for God? Plan on spending time with them this week.**

    _____

    _____

    _____

    _____

EPISODE 21

LIVING A LEGACY

How will people remember me? How will they remember you? Do people know I love Jesus and care about them too?

These are thought provoking questions and I admit I have thought about this many times as I have gotten older. In this video I share about a weatherman in our area who suddenly died. But he wasn't just a weatherman. Daily, for 30 years, he promoted different non-profit organizations and highlighted them. He had a tremendous impact on our community - attending local events, helping a kid learn to waterski. He was adored and had a deep commitment to our community. Many have said there will never be some-one who can fill his shoes. Now that is a legacy. So, how will people remember me?

I Thessalonians 5:11 tells us,

> *"Therefore encourage one another and build one another up, just as you also are doing."*

QUESTIONS

1. **Living a Godly legacy is pointing others to Christ. And for others to see that we love them no matter what; that we will share in their trials and joys. Psalm 34:3-5 says,**

   "Exalt the LORD with me, And let's exalt His name together. I sought the LORD and He answered me. And rescued me from all my fears. They looked to Him and were radiant, And their faces will never be ashamed."

   Does your face reflect the love of God? What kind of imprint will you have on someone's life? Can they tell that you care about them like Jesus does? What are some ways you can reflect God's love to others?

   _____

   _____

   _____

   _____

   _____

2. **Here is a list of some ways you can leave a legacy.**
   - ❖ Live like you mean it
   - ❖ Keep a journal
   - ❖ Share stories with your children
   - ❖ Be honest and stand for what is right
   - ❖ Give your family the gift of your time
   - ❖ Live for others and make sure they know they are important
   - ❖ Be an example

Can you add more to this list?

_____

_____

_____

_____

_____

_____

3. **I have children and grandchildren. The past few years I have been thinking more and more about all this. Matter fact, I feel a sense of urgency about their spiritual life more than ever. Not that I have not been concerned and prayed for them since they were in the womb, but I believe grandparents become more aware of our impact on our children and grandchildren as they grow older. Deuteronomy 6:6-7 states,**

> *"And these words, which I am commanding you today, shall be on your heart; and you shall teach them diligently to your sons and shall talk of them when you sit in your house and when you walk by the way and when you lie down and when you rise up."*

If you have not committed this to memory. Put it on your list. I am sure you have ideas of ways you could impact those around you. Write down 5 specific ways you can show Christ's love to someone in the upcoming months.

_____

_____

_____

_____

4. **Read Galatians chapter 6. It tells us to examine ourselves and share each others' loads. Then in verses 6-10 it tells us to do good to those in the household of faith. I love verse 9. Galatians 6:9:**

> *"Let us not lose heart in doing good, for in due time we will reap if we do not grow weary."*

We need patience in sowing good. Sometimes it can take years. Harvest does not come immediately. And sometimes we grow weary.

Write out Philippians 2:1-18. Verse 12 begins with "so then" - this is a great example of why you need to look at the context because the proceeding verses help us to understand the "why" of verses 12-18.

_____

_____

_____

_____

_____

_____

_____

_____

_____

Who is working?

_____

_____

5. *I am greatly encouraged by this passage. What encourages you?*

_____

_____

_____

_____

_____

6. **What do you want your legacy to be? How do you want to be remembered? Write down the things you do or want to do to show others that you care about them, to be understanding, and to make those in your life feel special?**

_____

_____

_____

_____

_____

_____

_____

_____

_____

_____

_____

_____

_____

_____

EPISODE 22

IT HAD TO BE

This video had been filmed Easter week, so it revolves around the events that lead up to the Resurrection. This is an important aspect of our faith to talk about any time of year, so let's take a look. As I have grown in my faith the past 45 years, I not only look at Palm Sunday as "the Kick-off" and The Cross and Resurrection as "the bookends," but I think about what happened in between. It was all perfectly planned and orchestrated by God. From the donkey being where it was supposed to be, to who would see Jesus first near the empty tomb, so many details were intricately planned out.

QUESTIONS

1. The term Passion is used to refer to the period of trials and suffering that Jesus experienced before His death. This term began to be used in the early 1300's. Even before Palm Sunday, things had been set in motion. Two months before, Jesus had raised Lazarus from the dead. This was one of the reasons the leaders wanted to kill Him, because so many people knew about it and were following Jesus. Because of this, Jesus and His followers stayed clear of Jerusalem until closer to Passover. Read and compare Zechariah 9:9-10 to Matthew 21:1-11 and Mark 11:1-11. How do these passages describe Jesus' entry into Jerusalem?

_____

_____

_____

_____

_____

_____

_____

Jesus was David's descendant becoming King of the Jews forever. Jesus riding on the foal of a donkey was an unmistakable fulfillment of God's Word, declaring to all that he is the rightful successor as King. Riding on a donkey was a symbol of meekness - prophesied hundreds of years before by Zechariah. People expected the Messiah would come to overthrow Rome by military force. Jesus came into the city from the east. The Roman procession was from the West. Jesus was the Messiah, but he did not come to overthrow Rome, but to reconcile all people to God through his death and resurrection.

2. On Monday they returned to Bethany which was a place where Jesus rested and gained His strength. He needed time to pray and be with HIs Father. Tuesday they went into the city early and did not return to Bethany until late. He had some run-ins with the Pharisees. They were trying to discredit Him. Read Matthew 21:12-17; Mark 11:15-33. What did the Pharisees have against Jesus?

_____

_____

_____

_____

_____

_____

3. Wednesday the record is silent. Most likely a day of prayer. Thursday we have the washing of the disciples feet and the last supper, betrayal, arrest. To follow in Jesus footsteps meant to love and show love in action. Love is always willing to serve. In sharing the bread and wine with Jesus (what we call "communion"), I am not sure how much the disciples fully understood. But they soon would. He who was to betray Jesus was revealed. Then they had time in the garden: sleeping, Jesus praying. He is under so much stress He is sweating blood. Read Luke 22:44-71. This is a lot to take in. Make a list of the events to help you visualize it.

_____

_____

_____

_____

_____

_____

_____

4. *As we consider the end of what we call "passion week", I would pray for all of us to not have "Easter" become rote for us. Each year we think about the crucifixion and also the Resurrection. They are ingrained in our Christian life, but we need to keep this fresh. We need to think about the pain and suffering Christ went through for you and for me. How do we do that? Maybe the same way we remember His birth. Many of us read Luke 2 sometime around Christmas. Right? You may even do it Christmas Eve.*

Read the passages about the last three days of Passion Week:

Matthew chapters 26-28

Mark chapters 14-16

Luke chapters 22-24

John chapters 18-20

This is a lot to read. Maybe read each gospel account on different days. Each has its own way of telling the account.

_____

_____

_____

_____

_____

_____

_____

_____

_____

_____

_____

5. *I think it is amazing that all these details were all planned out ahead and that Jesus knew what would happen every step of the way. What is the most impactful aspect of Passion Week to you?*

_____

_____

_____

_____

_____

_____

_____

_____

_____

_____

_____

_____

_____

_____

_____

_____

_____

_____

EPISODE 23

PREPARE YOUR MINDS FOR ACTION

Peter was the greatest leader of the early church. His name is mentioned more times than any other name in the Gospels except for Christ's.

Having been named "Simon" at birth, Jesus later changed Simon's name to Peter, meaning "the rock". Although he is often seen as impulsive and full of himself, it is that confidence and surety Jesus knew would see the early church through, as it was built. For He could not have used someone timid. He needed a person full of boldness and intentionality. Peter was a big factor in me writing my third book, "BOLD - Living Intentionally In Today's World". Now more than ever, we need Christians to stand up for their faith much like the first century Christians did.

QUESTIONS

1. After the ascension, Peter was the one to preach the sermon at Pentecost. He also began the process to choose the person to replace Judas. He is clearly the leader. Read 1 Peter 1. What is Peter trying to get across? Focus on verses 13-15. List 5 main points you see.

_____

_____

_____

_____

_____

_____

_____

2. In verses 22-25, he closes out the chapter by telling us to have a fervent love for our fellow believers from our heart, and that God's Word abides forever. It is the truth of the gospel that saves and the power of His Word does not fade away. So what does that mean for us? What occupies our heart?

_____

_____

_____

_____

_____

_____

3. Memorizing verses is a great way to keep God's Word in your heart and also helps you when you are sharing with someone. What are some of your favorites you have been memorizing? What method works best for you?

_____

_____

_____

_____

_____

_____

_____

_____

4. We need to prepare our mind for action. What do you fill your mind with? How much of your day is spent filling your mind with TV shows, movies, books, social media, or God's word, prayer, talking with other believers? Is there anything you need to cut back on or focus your mind on more?

_____

_____

_____

_____

_____

_____

_____

_____

5. Billy Graham said, "Do you want your faith to grow? Then let the Bible begin to saturate your mind and soul". Pray for God to help you spend time with Him. It is easy to let the day slip by. I pray in the morning but my favorite time to study is later in the day. My mind is not racing and I connect better. What about you? What is the best time for you to read God's Word?

_____

_____

_____

_____

_____

_____

_____

6. Keep your eyes fixed on Jesus and you will be ready to take action on all He has for you. Be inspired by others who are/ have been an example to you. Whether someone in the past or present, whose life has inspired and encouraged you to follow God?

_____

_____

_____

_____

_____

_____

_____

7. **Here are some verses on encouraging those around you.**

   Hebrews 10:24-25

   > *"And let us consider how to stimulate one another to love and good deeds, not forsaking our own assembling together, as is the habit of some, but encouraging one another; and all the more as you see the day drawing near."*

   1 Corinthians 16:13

   > *"Be on the alert, stand firm in the faith, act like men, be strong."*

   1 Thessalonians 5:11

   > *"Therefore, encourage one another and build one another up, just as you also are doing."*

EPISODE 24

PRACTICE THESE THINGS

We've been discussing what fuels our passion to serve others and encourage them to follow Christ. We abide in His Word and we prepare for action by doing what He calls us to do: to follow Him. Because we are human, we need to be reminded. Peter knew he would most likely die soon when he was writing 1 and 2 Peter. Christ had prophesied his death. Peter used these letters to serve as a permanent reminder of God's truths to Christians. So I am continually reminding all of you. The Bible never grows old. God does not change. Our calling does not stop.

QUESTIONS

1. **In 2 Peter we are encouraged to strive for moral excellence and to grow in Christian virtue. In chapter 1, verses 5-7 Peter tells us,**

   "Now for this very reason also, applying all diligence, in your faith supply moral excellence, and in your moral excellence, knowledge and in your knowledge, self-control, and in your self-control, perseverance, and in your perseverance, godliness, and in your godliness, brotherly kindness, and in your brotherly kindness, love."

   By doing these things we will shine Christ to others around us.

   Which of these traits will you work on this week? I have been working on kindness lately. Really trying to learn what it really means, and to practice it. By exhibiting these traits, others can see Christ in us. Write out some ways you can improve in the area you are concentrating on this week.

   _____

   _____

   _____

   _____

2. **Does it sometimes seem like we are going over and over the same concepts? Read 2 Peter 1:12-15:**

   "Therefore, I shall ALWAYS be ready to remind you of these things, even though you already know them, and have been established in the Truth which is present with you, and I consider it right, as long as I am in this earthly dwelling, to stir you up by way of reminder, knowing that the laying aside of my earthly

dwelling is imminent, as also our Lord Jesus Christ has made clear to me. And I will also be diligent that at any time after my departure you may be able to call these things to mind."

I am going to tell you a little story about when I was in college. I was attending Grace Community Church in Southern California. One of the summers I was there the pastor, John MacArthur, was gone for most of the summer. We were told he was touring around the US visiting churches and ministries and talking to people about his radio program, Grace to You. But when he returned, he did a 3 or 4 week sermon series on these verses. Why? Well, he had been at Grace for 11 years. He had gone through most of the Bible and thought maybe he had taught them all he could from scripture. Looking at these verses, he realized that everyone needs to be reminded about things they have already been taught.

How does this passage inspire you? What does it teach you about studying the Word?

_____

_____

_____

_____

_____

_____

So even if you have studied the Bible for years, or don't think there is anything new to learn, remember what you know! Those verses and passages you love and have learned from, can be read over and over and over. And God will continue to teach you through them.

3. **We need fellowship to stay in the Word. We need people to encourage us in Godly things. The Bible never grows old. Our calling does not stop. What helps you learn the Word? Do you underline? Do you take notes? If you are in a group study, share with each other these ideas.**

_____

_____

_____

4. **Ideas for action:**

   This is the challenge my LIVE BOLDLY Facebook group did last year. You could use a similar format or make up your own.

   ❖ **SUNDAYS** - Scriptures to read

   ❖ **MONDAYS** - Outline/memorize

   ❖ **TUESDAYS** - Take action

   ❖ **WEDNESDAYS** - Worship

   ❖ **THURSDAYS** - Family and friends

   ❖ **FRIDAYS** - Talk to God in prayer

   ❖ **SATURDAYS** - Service for others

Live Boldly - 30 Day Challenge

Month

_____

SUN	MON	TUE	WED	THU	FRI	SAT
	1 ☐ What verse encourages you to be BOLD	2 ☐ Walk with a neighbor	3 ☐ Prayers on Thankfulness	4 ☐ Meet with an unlikely friend	5 ☐ Pray to have passion for others	6 ☐ Help a widow or single parent
7 ☐ Read II Timothy 1:7	8 ☐ List 3 ways to meet someone new	9 ☐ Contact an old friend	10 ☐ Listen to your favorite worship song	11 ☐ Meet a new neighbor	12 ☐ Pray for ways to serve	13 ☐ Help someone with yardwork or a chore
14 ☐ Read I Peter 3:15-16	15 ☐ Favorite verse on serving others	16 ☐ Take a meal to someone	17 ☐ Pray attitudes of God	18 ☐ Take a church leader or pastor to lunch	19 ☐ Pray for people who need Christ	20 ☐ Treat someone to a fun activity (i.e. movie)
21 ☐ Read Rom 1:16	22 ☐ 3 ways to show kindness	23 ☐ Share your testimony with someone	24 ☐ Listen to a new song	25 ☐ Meet with a family member	26 ☐ Pray for family	27 ☐ Offer a service like babysitting or errands
28 ☐ Read II Cor 3:12	29 ☐ Memorize Prov 28:1	30 ☐ Tell someone you are praying for them	31 ☐ Worship in nature			

5. *I have a friend who passed away last year who was so inspiring to me. There was an older man who never talked to anyone. He was all alone. She decided she would go out to the mailbox every day when he did. He always went at the same time. She always waved and said hello. At first he just grunted or ignored her. Then one day he gave a little wave. Eventually he said hello. Perseverance. She also did a birthday party with the neighbors for an elderly woman who had no relatives in the area. These are wonderful ideas. And they do not take much effort. Who do you know that could use a little bit of joy this week? Make a plan today for what little way you could encourage them. Right now, write it down.*

_____

_____

_____

_____

_____

_____

_____

_____

_____

_____

_____

_____

_____

_____

EPISODE 25

DO YOU TRULY BELIEVE HE ANSWERS PRAYER

The next couple weeks we are going to be sharing some tidbits on prayer. This lesson will focus on faith.

Do you truly believe God can and will answer your prayers? Do you believe God does miracles?

QUESTIONS

1. **Hebrews 4:16**

    "Let us therefore draw near with confidence to the throne of grace, that we may receive mercy and may find grace to help in time of need."

    That word "confidence". Do you have confidence before God? Believers can come before God and speak openly and honestly without fear. 1 John 5:14-15,

    "and this is the confidence which we have before Him, that if we ask anything according to His will He hears us. And if we know that He hears us in whatever we ask, we know that we have the requests that we have asked from Him."

    What gives you assurance that He is listening?

    _____

    _____

    _____

    _____

    Do you feel confident that He will answer your prayer? What do you do if you don't?

    _____

    _____

    _____

    _____

2. *We should ask according to what the Bible teaches. God has greater wisdom and we can trust He knows best.*

   Look up the following verses. What is the idea in these verses?

   John 14:13-14 _____

   _____

   _____

   John 15:16 _____

   _____

   _____

   John 16:23 _____

   _____

   _____

   Matthew 7:11 _____

   _____

   _____

   Psalm 145:18 _____

   _____

   _____

   Which one(s) encourage you the most? Why?

   _____

   _____

   _____

3. **There are many aspects to prayer. Here are some ways you can pray:**

   ❖ **Pray God's attributes:** He never changes, all powerful, holy, wise, loving, faithful, good, etc.

   ❖ **Share your heart:** the fear, the disappointment, the anger, the joy, etc.

   ❖ **Ask forgiveness**

   ❖ **Praise God:** Thank Him for the big and small things

   ❖ **Pray with a friend**

   ❖ **Pray scripture**: use the words of a verse to pray for someone or yourself

   ❖ **Pray with hope**

   ❖ **Pray in God's will**

   Are some of these ways new to you? Which ones?
   What new way to pray will you try this week?

   _____

   _____

   _____

   _____

4. *In the video I mention the book, <u>A Severe Mercy</u> by Sheldon Vanauken. I have given this book to many people through the years. The book has two main themes that I see. One is that an unbelieving young couple goes to Oxford and they do not understand how someone as brilliant as C. S. Lewis could believe in Christianity. The other is that once they become believers, events take place where hard things happen to bring them closer to God. Even though we are Christians, that does not mean we won't experience hardship. Which is why it is mentioned in this lesson. WE do not know what is best but WE have a sovereign God who wants to listen to us and who does grant us more than we deserve. We need to come before Him trusting and believing in His wonder-working power. Fully trusting in His answer and that it is best.*

Read Romans 8:26-30.

"In the same way the Spirit also helps our weakness; for we do not know how to pray as we should, but the Spirit Himself intercedes for us with groanings too deep for words; and He who searches the hearts knows what the mind of the Spirit is, because He intercedes for the saints according to the will of God. And we know that God causes all things to work together for good to those who love God, to those who are called according to His purpose. For those whom He foreknew, He also predestined to become conformed to the image of His Son, so that He would be the firstborn among many brethren; and these whom He predestined, He also called; and these whom He called, He also justified; and these whom He justified, He also glorified."

How do you know God is working for your good? What do you do when you don't feel like good things are happening?

_____

_____

_____

_____

_____

_____

_____

_____

5. *God doesn't always answer in ways we expect. Can you think of a time when you prayed for one thing, and God answered in a different, better way? Or a time when you prayed for a specific thing, that in hindsight, would have not been good for you, and thankfully God did not grant? What did that teach you about God, about yourself, about prayer?*

_____

_____

_____

_____

_____

_____

_____

_____

_____

_____

_____

_____

_____

_____

_____

_____

EPISODE 26

WHEN YOU SEEK ME

Last chapter we discussed that God does answer prayer. He can do all things. It may not be your timeline or how you thought He would answer but you can trust Him to answer. This lesson has me thinking that believing is great but you also need to seek Him. Spend time with Him and share with Him. It is true that He knows all things. But He desires our communion with Him.

QUESTIONS

1. **Let's begin by reading James 5:13-16:**

   "Is anyone among you suffering? Let him pray. Is anyone cheerful? Let him sing praises. Is anyone among you sick? Let him call for the elders of the church, and let them pray over him, anointing him with oil in the name of the Lord; and the prayer offered in faith will restore the one who is sick, and the Lord will raise him up, and if he has committed sins, they will be forgiven him. Therefore, confess your sins to one another, and pray for one another, so that you may be healed. The effective prayer of a righteous man can accomplish much."

   We need an active faith. As you can see from this passage, prayer and singing are coupled together. You are not lamenting somewhere hoping that something will just happen. You are being active by praying. What are three things you can actively pray or praise God for this week? Write them out. Writing things down solidifies the idea in your mind.

   _____

   _____

   _____

2. **In James 5:16, prayer can accomplish much. God wants us to share our inner-most thoughts with Him. I sometimes pray when taking a bath, sounds crazy but I do and I usually cry, they are my heavy burdens. Do you think things are too difficult for God? Do you share your deepest burdens? What are you passionate about? Are your prayers fervent? How can you pray more fervently?**

_____

_____

_____

_____

_____

3. **Read Jeremiah 29. It is always good to take in the context but we will focus on the familiar passage in verses 11-13. Jeremiah was known as the weeping prophet. He was put in stocks being charged as a false prophet. He was thrown into a pit, forced to flee and he also predicted the Babylonian captivity. He lived life in conflict. Yet he told of God's blessings and peace for Israel's future, and he shared what God planned to do. This gives us great hope.**

> " 'For I know the plans that I have for you,' declares the LORD, 'plans for welfare and not for calamity to give you a future and a hope. Then you will call upon Me and come and pray to Me, and I will listen to you. And you will seek Me and find Me, when you search for Me with all your heart.' "

4. **God wants us to call on Him. Write out a prayer right now for the greatest burden on your heart. Even if it is someone or something you have prayed for over and over again for years. Pray with hope.**

_____

_____

_____

_____

_____

_____

5. Here is a quote from John Bunyan, "Prayer is a sincere, sensible, affectionate pouring our heart or soul to God, through Christ, in the strength and assistance of the Holy Spirit, for such things as God has promised, or according to the Word of God, for the good of the Church, with submission in faith to the will of God." Nothing is too big or too small. Just have sweet communion with Him. Read the following verses. What do they say about prayer?

Philippians 4:6 _____

_____

_____

Mark 11:24 _____

_____

_____

Romans 8:26 _____

_____

_____

Matthew 6:6 _____

_____

_____

James 5:16 _____

_____

_____

Matthew 26:41 _____

_____

_____

*1 Thessalonians 5:16-18*_____

_____

_____

6. Which of these verses inspire or encourage you? Why?

_____

_____

_____

_____

_____

_____

_____

7. The following verses may encourage you when your heart is heavy.

Psalm 55:22

> *"Cast your burden upon the LORD and He will sustain you; He will never allow the righteous to be shaken."*

Psalm 94:19

> *"When my anxious thoughts multiply within me, Your consolations delight my soul."*

Romans 8:6

> *"For the mind set on the flesh is death, but the mind set on the Spirit is life and peace."*

What is your favorite Psalm? Mine is Psalm 37. Verses 23-24
mention God not letting us fall because He is the one who
holds our hand. When I was a new believer my dad had just
died. I did not know much about the Bible but I just kept read-
ing Psalms. They gave me comfort. Glance through the Psalms
and choose your favorite - maybe there are three or more!
Write them down.

_____

_____

_____

_____

_____

_____

_____

_____

_____

_____

_____

EPISODE 27

YOUR PRAYER LIFE

When we pray, we are not limited to what kind of request or how many. God wants us to share our hearts each day, multiple times a day.

Ephesians 6:18 says,

> *"With all prayer and petition pray at all times in the Spirit, and with this in view, be on the alert with all perseverance and petition for all the saints."*

The last couple lessons have discussed whether we believe He answers us, and about seeking Him. But do not be concerned about how often or what you ask. Well, within reason. Ask in His name and don't ask for something He wouldn't want you to have. But do not hesitate to share what is on your heart. Even if we do not understand how to pray for something, He understands us. Trust and believe.

QUESTIONS

1. *Several years ago someone gave me a book by Jodie Berndt. I had some other books about praying scripture, but had not delved too much into them at the time. I was going through a heartbreaking time and read this book over and over, underlining and filling in blanks with names. That book is worn with tattered pages. You can do this with many scriptures and you don't need a book to help you. My moma used to pray through our church directory. Even though she did not know everyone listed there. When she would finish, she would start again. Write down some ways you pray for individuals. What helps you stay on track with your prayer list?*

   _____

   _____

   _____

   _____

2. *God loves us and He is sovereign. This is so encouraging to me. Pray with hope instead of doubt. Read Mark 11:22-24. What are the key words that stand out to you? Read it again and look for these words and phrases: Have faith, believe, no doubt, ask, believe, it will be yours. What stands out to you?*

   _____

   _____

   _____

   _____

   _____

   _____

3. *Read Jeremiah 29:11-13 again. What plans does God have for you?*

_____

_____

_____

_____

_____

How should knowing God's plans for you affect your prayer life?

_____

_____

_____

_____

_____

_____

4. *A tool I have used as I pray is the acronym "ACTS". Pray in this order:*

❖ **Adoration:** give praise to God for who He is and what He has done

❖ **Confession:** tell God about all your sins - large and small

❖ **Thanksgiving:** thank God for things, specific things, not just in general

❖ **Supplication:** ask God to work in your life or the lives of others

You may feel awkward praying like this at first, but as you practice, it will become easier. Read Matthew 6:9-13 - the Lord's Prayer has many of these elements in it.

5. **Other tools you can use when you pray are:**

❖ **Journaling** - write a letter to God: this gives you time to think about your words and gives you clarity.

❖ **Pray with a partner** - praying with another person keeps you focused and regular in your prayer time

❖ **Pray through a list** - make lists of people and things to pray for (work, friends, relatives, church, missions, etc). You don't need to pray about everything everytime! Use different lists on different days.

❖ **Read through Psalms** - pray about those things the Psalmist prays about

Which prayer practice will you try out this week?

_____

_____

_____

_____

_____

_____

_____

_____

_____

_____

_____

_____

_____

_____

EPISODE 28

SACRIFICIAL SERVICE

I was looking at

Ephesians 6:7,

> *"With goodwill render service,*
> *as to the Lord and not to people".*

I love Paul's letters to the churches. And this letter to Ephesus is no exception. The first three chapters emphasize Christian doctrine and the last three talk about our behavior. He encourages us to remember our great blessings and to be of help to others; not to be complacent but to put on the whole armor of God, and go forth and be vigilant. Verse seven is telling us to remember who we are working FOR, not men but God Himself.

QUESTIONS

1. Corrie ten Boom was a faithful hero of the faith. My moma had one of her books on her nightstand that she read with her Bible and Our Daily Bread every night until she died. Here is a very brief overview of Corrie ten Boom's life.

   Corrie ten Boom's family were watchmakers in the Netherlands. There were four children. When World War II grew worse, and it was clear people were being taken to concentration camps and killed, the ten Boom family built a hidden room in their house. There they could hide people from the Nazis. It is estimated that they were able to save approximately 800 Jewish people. Her sister Betsy, their father and Corrie were eventually taken to a concentration camp. Their father and Betsy ended up dying there, but Corrie lived through that and went on to share Christ, travel and write books. She was also a watchmaker. She helped many people deal with psychological issues that resulted from the war. Corrie shared that no matter your circumstances there is always the hope that God gives us. Here are a few quotes from her.

   > "Any concern too small
   > to be turned into prayer is too small
   > to be made into a burden."

   > "Let God's promises
   > shine on your problems"

   > "Never be afraid
   > to trust an unknown future
   > to a KNOWN God."

   Share the one obstacle or difficult circumstance you are trying to overcome right now.

   _____

   _____

   _____

   _____

   _____

2. **God is preparing us through our trials for the work He is going to give us to do. Corrie ten Boom used her past experiences to encourage and help others. What trials have you been through that God has used in developing your faith, character or future? Have you heard of other people who have been through difficult experiences who used them to help others? How does overcoming these past trials encourage you or encourage others?**

_____

_____

_____

_____

3. **I often think of the disciples and the sacrifices they made by leaving their life behind to truly follow Christ. Matthew 4:19 gives us Jesus' call to Peter and Andrew, who I am sure had no idea what the future held at that point.**

> *"And He said to them, 'Follow Me, and I will make you fishers of men.'*

What is He calling you to do for Him right now? Is there a friend or family member you are sharing the gospel with? Are you taking care of a person in need?

1 Peter 2:21 states,

> *"For you have been called for this purpose, since Christ also suffered for you, leaving you an example for you to follow in His steps."*

_____

_____

_____

_____

4. In the first few chapters of this workbook, I encouraged you to write out your testimony; your story and journey of how God has worked in your life. God wants us to use things in our life (things he has brought us through) to encourage other believers to live intentionally so they can share the gospel with others too. Do you have a dramatic life-changing type of testimony? Or has your life's journey been one of gradual and steady faith? God uses both to bring others to salvation, and to encourage the faith of believers. You don't need a "fancy" testimony - God has given you YOUR life, your journey to share with others, believers and unbelievers. What part of your journey can you share with someone this week?

_____

_____

_____

_____

_____

_____

_____

_____

5. Read Isaiah 55. Then look at verse 12 again.

   "For you will go out with joy, and be led forth with peace; The mountains and the hills will break forth into shouts of joy before you, and all the trees of the field will clap their hands."

EPISODE 29

GIVING YOUR LIFE

"Sometimes...fear does not subside and...
one must choose to do it afraid."
ELISABETH ELLIOT

This chapter will share about Jim and Elisabeth Elliot. Theirs is a story of great courage and boldness of faith. Not all of us can go to a dangerous place and share the Lord, but we have all experienced our heart pounding when sharing our faith with a loved one who we felt might be antagonistic toward what we believe, or maybe a friend who has been asking questions. As we grow in our faith, we are given more and more opportunities to share. I encourage you to prepare yourself for such times. I hope this lesson will show you that it is time for you to move forward in your life of faith.

QUESTIONS

1. Jim and Elisabeth Elliot had gone to language school in 1952 to study Spanish. They felt God had given them an urgent desire to share the gospel. They went to a tribe in Ecuador. They spent three years sharing their faith with the Quechua Indians. Many had come to Christ and were growing in their faith. Jim had heard of a tribe, not far away, that was so dangerous no one would go there. The Huaorani people were called Auca ("savages") by the Quechua. Jim felt more and more burdened to go. They were working with four other missionary couples and they decided to reach out. Have you had a time in your life where God has pushed you to move ahead with something you feel scared to do? How did you respond?

_____

_____

_____

_____

_____

_____

_____

_____

_____

_____

_____

_____

2. Nate Saint was a missionary pilot on their team. The group decided to lower gifts onto a beach near the Auca/Huaorani tribe.

After a couple of months of leaving gifts, the tribe sent back a package. The missionaries decided that now was the time to finally make personal contact. The missionaries landed on a beach and set up camp. After a few days, a few tribe members came, shared a meal and a plane ride. Several days later warriors came with spears and killed all 5 men. Operation Auca was not a failure. Many in the tribe later became believers. Two years later Elisabeth and Nate's sister went back to live in the village. The Aucas had become a friendly tribe. What are your thoughts on this? Do you see how God worked? Do you think any of the missionaries' actions were unwise? Do you believe they were following God's direction even though it led to their deaths?

_____

_____

_____

_____

_____

_____

3. *Even though difficult things happened to her (husband murdered, single mom, living in a foreign land), Elisabeth followed God's calling for her life and ministered to the Huaorani people, and later through radio, books and speaking events encouraged others to follow God's leading in their lives. Have you had difficult things happen in your life that seem to derail you from following God? What do you think He wants you to do now?*

_____

_____

_____

_____

_____

_____

4. **Elisabeth became one of the most influential women of the twentieth century. She wrote many books and spoke to thousands. She inspired many, and people are still encouraged by her and Jim's testimony and faithfulness to God. She listened to God's voice and followed through on what God told her to do. Look up the following verses on listening to God.**

*Luke 11:28*_____

_____

_____

*Jeremiah 33:3*_____

_____

_____

*1 John 5:14*_____

_____

_____

*Psalm 116:1-2*_____

_____

_____

*Matthew 7:24*_____

_____

_____

*Romans 10:17*_____

_____

_____

5. **What are things we can do to grow in our ability to step out in faith with purpose? Read the following verses. What do they say we should do? What will God do?**

Psalm 31:24 _____

_____

_____

Hebrews 10:24-25 _____

_____

_____

Psalm 121:1-2 _____

_____

_____

1 Corinthians 16:13 _____

_____

_____

Romans 8:31 _____

_____

_____

2 Timothy 1:7 _____

_____

_____

EPISODE 30

WITH A LOUD VOICE

*"Being a Christian is more than
just an instantaneous conversion-
it is a daily process
whereby you grow to be
more and more like Christ"*

BILLY GRAHAM

Billy Graham was one of the most influential people of the twentieth century. It is calculated that he preached to 210 million people in his lifetime in more than 185 countries. Gallup's poll has had him on their list of most admired men 61 times, which is a record. His goal was to reach as many people as possible with the gospel. Recently this has become more and more important to me. I may not reach millions but I feel that sense of urgency.

QUESTIONS

1. When Billy Graham was 28 years old, he preached his first ser-
    mon to a large crowd of 6,000. Twenty-eight is young. No matter
    your age, God has a plan of how He will use you. Have you had
    ideas, dreams, or hopes of ways He could use you that you are
    not already involved with? Maybe you are working in several min-
    istries already but feel you are being prodded to do something
    different. Maybe you are confident you are right where God
    wants you. Look up the following verses. What do they tell you?

    Colossians 3:23-24 _____

    _____

    _____

    John 13:12-14_____

    _____

    _____

    1 Peter 4:10 _____

    _____

    _____

    Matthew 9:37-38_____

    _____

    _____

    Mark 8:35 _____

    _____

    _____

2. *Billy Graham asked, "Do you want your faith to grow? Then let the Bible begin to saturate your mind and soul." If you too want your faith to grow, how are you immersing your mind and soul in the Bible? What have you done or are doing to know what the Bible says? Is there something more that you should be doing?*

_____

_____

_____

_____

_____

_____

3. *Throughout these videos we have given you tools on sharing your faith with others. Let's review - Write out your testimony in short form so that you will plant it firmly into your mind and be able to recall it quickly when you have the opportunity. Have 3-4 verses memorized to be able to share. Go over the basic concepts: God, sin, Jesus died on the cross, faith and acceptance.*

_____

_____

_____

_____

_____

_____

_____

4. **Pray for opportunity. Pray for God to work in your heart and give you a heart for those who do not have a relationship with God: Friends, family and even the rude person you don't care for. THEY ALL NEED JESUS. Pray now for those who need Christ that you may be able to share with them soon.**

_____

_____

_____

_____

_____

_____

_____

5. **Sometimes it is scary to talk to that person about Christ, take that step into a new ministry, or give up your current lifestyle for a new venture. But remember the disciples? They instantly quit what they were doing, and they followed Christ. Is there something the Holy Spirit has laid on your heart lately? A relative who needs Christ, a prodigal? A refugee family in your neighborhood? A mission trip? Write down three possibilities that have been on your mind lately. They may be extreme or may be simple. Pray that God would direct you.**

_____

_____

_____

_____

_____

_____

PERSONAL NOTES

PERSONAL NOTES

PERSONAL NOTES

PERSONAL NOTES

_____

_____

_____

_____

_____

_____

_____

_____

_____

_____

_____

_____

_____

_____

_____

_____

_____

_____

ABOUT THE AUTHOR

Nicki Corinne White has a passion for studying and teaching God's Word. She has been leading Bible studies and discipling young women for many years . She is very involved in her local church with both children's ministry and women's ministry. She has a tender heart for those who are hurting and those who are new to church. Nicki hopes to be an encouragement to those around her: lending a listening ear, kind word or a Biblical reminder. She also opens her home to share and serve others through hospitality on a regular basis, and believes we are all called to do this. Nicki feels blessed to have been able to use her story and personal experience to encourage others and hopes to expand this ministry through her writing.

Nicki Corinne grew up in Snohomish, Washington, with her mom, dad and sister. She was adopted at the age of one with her sister, Lisa, into the Maynard family. Nicki went to college at a small Christian Liberal Arts College in Southern California. She met her husband, Craig, after graduating and was married two years later. They moved to the central coast of California, then on to the Bay Area where they had their first three children. Five years later, they moved to Boise, Idaho where their fourth child was born. Nicki has worked several jobs including teaching, merchandising, administrative work, and various artist projects. She enjoys spending time outdoors, painting, writing, and spending time with her four children and seven grandkids.

Nicki Corinne has published three books: "Not Really a Princess", "It's Not About The Pie", and "Bold: Living Intentionally in Today's World". She also has published the first volume of "LIVE BOLDLY WORKBOOK" for video episodes 1-15. She looks forward to sharing this second workbook with you and others to complement the video series "LIVE BOLDLY".

CONTACT US

Nicki Corinne White is available for book signings and speaking engagements. To get in touch with her team, please email us or message us through her website.

Email:

nickicorinnewhite@gmail.com

Website:

www.liveboldlyministries.com

Social Media:

Facebook Instagram Twitter YouTube

Find all the videos for this workbook on YouTube @nickicorinnewhite7299 (episodes 16-30)